# SINGLE YOUNG AND SINGLE MUM

WRITTEN BY
LEE-ANNE SCHONIAN

Copyright © 2018 Lee-Anne Schonian

All rights reserved. No part of this book may be used or reproduced in any manner whatsoever withour prior written consent of the author, except as provided by the Australian copyright law.

First published in Australia 2018
by Karen Mcdermott
www.karenmcdermott.com.au

National Library of Australia Cataloguing-in-Publisher data:

ISBN 978-0-6482127-3-7

Designer: Parklife Group Pty Ltd™
www.parklifegroup.com.au

*To all the mamas out there.
This one is for you!*

# *You will be ok*

These four words are expected to magically alleviate all our pain and problems. If you've been hearing that sentence more often than usual, you're probably ready to pull your hair out while you curl up in a ball under your covers sobbing away to Adele but trying not to get your mascara all over your clean bed sheets. Truth is, you will have many days and nights like this. Your heart feels like it's been stabbed a thousand times. So many thoughts rush through your head and you're not sure whether to pay attention to them or block them out. After you've stopped crying, you lie staring at the ceiling/walls wondering what you ever did to deserve this.

Single mother life does not discriminate, and to top it all off, everything that can possibly go wrong probably will until you find yourself here, broken and distraught from the outburst of emotional trauma. During this moment, you will be left with nothing but the unpleasant realisation you are broken and not coping – and that's OK. Allow yourself to feel the pain you're experiencing and accept that you are hurt. The realisation that you are a single mum is not an easy pill to swallow and let's be honest, who wants to parent alone. These are circumstances you cannot control. The only thing you can control is how you deal with it.

What am I supposed to do with myself now? Nothing. The answer is nothing. Be broken. Embrace that pain because it will become your power. Without pain we will never grow, self-improvement will never be achieved. Do not stress about the judgment of others, which will only increase your anxiety. We always believe that experiencing emotional pain requires some sort of immediate rescue plan in order to stop the hurt. Wrong. Masking your pain is only temporary. Whether you mask it with someone else, alcohol, medication or some weird habit, the sorrow you avoided and failed to deal with properly will always be there, lingering in the back of your unconscious mind, waiting to make its debut, usually during a mental breakdown performance.

Remember to focus on the 'now' and not worry about the future until you have come to terms with your current situation. Whether we like it or not the 'single mum' title always carries a sense of pity or negative judgment, as if we are less worthy because we parent alone. This is especially the case if you are a young mother under the age of twenty-five. At this age, a lot of your close friends don't have kids because they're too busy partying, travelling Europe and planning where to take their next Instagram upload. They are unable to relate to such situations because they don't have a clue what parenting entails, which will leave you feeling lost and lonely. It doesn't help when they try give you advice about single parenting…

Whether your single-mother situation is a result of a man walking out on you or his mistreatment, always remember that people who cause others pain usually are suffering themselves. Never use the wrong someone did to you as a reflection of yourself or your sense of self-worth. Be broken, let the tears flow. Have days where you leave the house messy, stay in PJs all day and eat takeaway for a week straight, watch The Notebook while trying to juggle mother duties in between. Try not to go out getting 'wasted' and make bad decisions because you'll only end up paying for it the next day.

As a single mother, you will be left fighting for yourself. Not physically, but mentally. Your confidence, self-esteem and self-worth has taken a beating. As mothers do, we will always put our children before ourselves, which means most of the time we are left on the back burner. There's no denying that we are all envious of the mother who drops her kids off at daycare with a fresh blow dry, a body that looks like it walked off the runway, and who seems to have her sh*t together.

# TAKE NOTE

"You were born to live beautifully, not broken"

# BE
## BROKEN

It's easier said than done and I know this first hand. Many of us tend to become that woman who will deny till you die rather than admit she is hurting, and when people ask if you're OK, you nod your head and hope they don't notice the slightly forced smile. It is not easy and you will find yourself repeatedly taking two steps forward and three steps back until you can learn how to accept it. All negative thoughts that could possibly exist in the human mind will run through your head and you will start questioning yourself on every aspect of your life. Am I even a good person? I know that thought ran through my head multiple times. Whether single parenting is new for you or has been your situation for a while, being profoundly affected by the reality that you are parenting on your own is not a sign of weakness. You do not need to be ashamed that things did not work out the way you wanted them to.

The biggest struggle most single mums will encounter during this soul-draining moment is parenting. I am not going to give you any parenting advice because, I wing every single damn day of motherhood and half the time I don't even know what I am doing. Does anyone really? I once told my work colleague that as long as my child is fed, clothed and breathing, I believe I am doing a great job. She laughed it off and thought I was joking but that's all I was capable of at that point. Most days you will find yourself being set off by the smallest things. You will be forgetful, your mind will be cloudy and you're going to be so unreliable that you can't even commit to replying to a text message. So when you walk into your house and forget you had a rent inspection that morning, fall to your knees and bawl your eyes out in the kitchen, it's OK, your life is not over. You are hurting and you need to allow yourself to do so. Let that nauseating pain travel through your entire body so you never forget it.

Some people need to break themselves over and over again until they finally accept they are broken and decide to endure the pain. It's intriguing that our thinking pattern has become so toxic over time that we tend to believe that if we are vulnerable and hurt, it is not OK. It is normal. Have you ever met one of those people who are full of wisdom, who carry themselves with confidence and are the most humble person that ever existed? Their peaceful, stress-free aura consumes your mind with a twist of envy and jealousy. I have, and I thought, 'How come this person was blessed with such a problem-free life?' And that thought, that judgment, is usually so far from the truth.

The wisest, most kind-hearted and peaceful people are usually the ones that have experienced the most pain and heartbreak throughout the course of their life. They are the ones that have fallen down repeatedly and got back up again. They have been dragged through the dirt (maybe not literally), rejected, heart-broken and left to learn how to fight for themselves, which is why they are able to appreciate the smallest things in life. To be wise, you must be educated; and what better way to be educated than to experience setbacks first hand. Spiritual and emotional growth don't come from joy but from genuine sadness.

Take the time to acknowledge that there are people in your life who are going to hurt you, and who probably have hurt you…a lot. Whether they do it intentionally or not doesn't make your pain any less. It has a greater effect when we are hurt by our significant other. We spend hours, months, even years, analysing the situation, trying to figure out the whys and what ifs. People are selfish, they are not always going to take into consideration your feelings and how their behaviour will impact you. You can do back-flips for a man (rephrase: boy) who wouldn't even lift a finger for you and that has nothing to do with you or your worth. That is a reflection of them and who they are as a person. We always think that losing someone who doesn't appreciate you and hurts you is a loss, when really it is a gain. All they would ever do is drag you down and drain all of your positive energy. Let them go, and don't keep going back to what broke you. You would rather be alone and hurting than with someone who doesn't care whether you're there or not. Sometimes we just have to leave the past behind and keep going. We can't change our circumstances; we have to learn to accept what is and what was.

"Just because he hates himself, does not mean that pouring more of your love his way will fix him. It will only leave you emptier."

Mark my words, if he cheated on you, he will do it again and also to the next person. It's a statistic that men who have cheated before are much more likely to cheat again. It is a big step to take, admitting to yourself that you've been cheated on and you got hurt. Do not defend his actions or make excuses for him. You are only fooling yourself. Being hurt by someone shows that you cared and that is nothing to be ashamed of. Honour your feelings and experience your emotional pain. By bottling up tears, you are bottling up negative energy and you no longer have room for that in your life.

If he moves on to another relationship as if you never existed, do not let that have an impact on you. It's like rubbing salt into the wound but he is only going to do to her what he did to you, and all those disgusting habits he has are still there! You've had that experience, you know what it's like to be in a relationship with him and you know what? It isn't for you. Be thankful you are no longer in that situation and send his new partner all the love and strength in the world (she's probably going to need it to survive). Leave him and any other soul-draining asshole in the past and never look back. Deny them the power to hurt you anymore. You're moving onto bigger and better things.

"Do not dwell in the past. The past doesn't have your healing, the future does"

Always keep in mind that your current situation is not your final destination; it is just a chapter in your life. This chapter is temporary, it is part of the process and it will not last forever. In twelve months, you will be in a completely different situation, with completely different problems. Once you have welcomed the emotions you are feeling and have stopped trying to hide or push them away, you will begin the healing process. Whether that means crying in the shower while your three-year-old bangs on the bathroom door wondering if you've drowned in your own self-pity – so be it. Be broken and own it. Do not be that drug addict that continues to deny they have a problem until they end up overdosing and in ICU– OK that was a bit dramatic, but you get the drift. Acknowledgment and acceptance is the key to moving forward. Moving on doesn't mean you're giving up, it just means you are choosing happiness over hurt.

TAKE NOTE

# BE
## BROKEN

# WARNING! RANT AHEAD

Use this section to debrief. Write down your feelings and thoughts on your current situation:

# WEEK 1

# WEEK 2

# WEEK 3

# WEEK 4

# WEEK 5

# WEEK 6

# WEEK 7

# WEEK 8

# WEEK 9

# WEEK 10

# WEEK 11

# WEEK 12

# SUMMARY

# THE
## HEALING

Post mental-breakdown at work (yes, at work), I found myself sitting at the traffic lights staring blankly ahead at the road in front of me. Why did I still feel this way? It had been months of feeling like a fragile charity case, filled with anxiety and ready to explode into tears at any moment. All the energy I had left in my entire body was being put into raising a child, trying to be a half-decent parent. The sound of my alarm each morning was still awakening me to the reality that this was not a dream, and all my problems were real.

Sometimes it takes the most uncomfortable road to lead you to the most beautiful places and you will never understand the purpose of your pain until you conquer the struggle. Healing is all about accepting the changes in your life and adapting to the new normal. Everybody's circumstances are different and your life will continue to change as long as you continue to grow. You can't let what's difficult to do keep you from doing what you need to do.

Healing is not an overnight process and it doesn't help that most of us do not allow ourselves to properly heal after an emotionally traumatic event, which is why it takes longer. Everybody is different and healing times will vary. We all find our turning point eventually and unfortunately for me, my turning point was losing one of my best friends. Since that day, I have never been ungrateful for hearing that annoying alarm each morning as I am able to drag my ass out of bed. Your children have a mother, and you have been blessed with another day. Be grateful. Stop admiring someone else's life you wish you had and you will find yourself on the road to having that life.

If you haven't already, you will come to realise that your life will never evolve or change until you make a change in what you're doing. Nobody can help you, only you can help yourself. Girlfriends can give you advice on what to do and probably will, but not only will you pick up the Askhole title, you will most likely continue in your vicious self-pity cycle until you decide you're ready for change.

What is an Askhole? A person who constantly asks for advice yet does the opposite every time. You can stay broken, fragile and anxiety ridden or you can decide enough is enough, and that life is not for you because you can do better and you deserve better. Not only is it about you, but your children. You will find that instead of screaming at them because they continue to bite each apple and put it back in the fruit bowl, you let it slide over your head and walk away. As a single mother, in her twenties, it is quite intimidating to think about the future, and even worse, dating. Do I even remember how to flirt? Probably not, and are you ready for that? I highly doubt it. This moment is all about you. You need to focus on giving yourself what you need to heal your spirit, your mind and your heart.

*"It is hard to find healing when you're trying to find closure, and really the only closure you need is to understand that you deserve better."*

Thoughts play a huge role in our quality of life. Thoughts turn into beliefs and those beliefs are reflected in our behavior. If you can control your thinking, you will be able to control the quality of your life. You won't be able to control what comes into your mind but you can choose the thoughts to hold onto and put energy into. So those negative, meaningless and dumb thoughts that drag you down are the ones to let come in and flow straight out of your head. What you think about, you put energy into and what you put energy into will grow. Time usually is the essence of our pain. Thoughts about the past, and what was, what happened and what should have happened will only ever bring you down. Peace is something you will never experience if you keep letting the uncontrollable things control you. The only thing we can ever control is now.

If you're like me and can hold a grudge for a lifetime towards people who have done you wrong, you will need to learn how to let go. As the legendary Martin Luther King said, 'Darkness cannot drive out darkness; only light can do that. Hate cannot drive out hate: only love can do that'. Do not let the wrong someone did to you create darkness in your life. They do not deserve that power. Healing is about acceptance. Acceptance of your life as it is. All the pain you've endured, the grief, the stress and the struggle. Just remember, people are built from every mistake they've ever made.

It is difficult for us to move forward in our lives and heal ourselves when we hold onto people or situations that are the cause of our pain. If your life is filled with negativity, there is no room for positive change. You need to make room for your future by removing everything in your life that no longer serves you or supports your growth. Removing sources of pain will allow your heart to begin to mend, and I encourage you to do things that continually feed that healing. It is a wonderful feeling when you begin to experience days without pain and heartache. It does get easier and you get stronger each day that passes. The pain will become less and its power over you will diminish. As you are still hurting and still healing, you need to protect yourself. Protect your energy. If you're an empath, your soft and forgiving nature will tend to attract narcissistic parasites that are drawn to the light that shines from you. If you have to close yourself off to situations, people or social media to protect yourself, then do it. Even though you may seem like an arrogant asshole, it doesn't matter. You are all that matters right now. Deleting spree, here you come!

It's a daunting thought to be alone. You see all these people and their sickening love posts about how perfect they are for each other. Social media creates false representations of reality and unfortunately young women are out there comparing themselves to a lifestyle that doesn't exist. Everything visible is fake, everything invisible is real. So why are we so afraid to be alone and happy? I will never forget the quote, 'Some people are so afraid of being alone they accept the Devil as a mate and pretend to be happy'. It all comes with the perception that in order to be 'settled down' and happy, you need to have a companion. This is so far from reality, it is possible to be settled in your life and be happy without having a significant other. A lot of women stay in unhealthy and abusive relationships because they are so afraid to stand alone, or consider themselves validated because they have someone. They become used to being treated a certain way and settle for less because they are so conditioned to believe that is all they are worth.

Being alone and happy takes strength and determination. It will help you to discover yourself and not be defined by someone else. You won't have time for anyone else's problems because you're too busy being in a relationship with yourself. You can't f*ck with someone that is not afraid to be alone, because you will lose every single time. And who the hell wants to share their hard- earned money? Who wants to care about how they look in the morning or whether they need to put clothes on when they do the backyard gardening? Definitely not me. It takes a strong person to remain single in a society that is so accustomed to settling with anything just to say they have something. Being alone is uncomfortable but it is necessary for you to heal.

"Healing doesn't mean the damage never existed, it means the damage no longer controls our lives."

# TAKE NOTE

# MY
## DAILY
### AFFIRMATIONS

I deserve to be happy just as much as anyone else.

I welcome my emotions and honour the way I am feeling.

I believe in myself and in my ability to succeed.

I do not need anyone else in my life to be happy.

Everything is going to work out for my highest good.

I release the drama of my past as I consciously create my future.

I approve of myself and love myself as I am, all of me.

The pain I am feeling cannot be compared to the joy thats coming.

There is gold in every problem. I know challenges are here to serve me.

Today is a brand new day. My past does not define my future.

I will not focus on things that cannot be changed or controlled.

I have the power to create the life I want to live for myself and my children.

I am strong enough to stand on my own.

I am enough.

# FINDING YOU

"I understood myself only after I destroyed myself, and only in the process of fixing myself did I know who I really was."

Everyone always talks about 'finding yourself' as if you can have a long bath, put on a face mask and go on a week trip to Bali and it will be done. Who even has time to have a bath anyway? I sure can't, not without a mini version of myself standing there staring at me as if I'm some sort of sea animal. Basically, it's all about finding out what makes you laugh, what makes you feel empowered and strong, what your demons are and what you're passionate about. Once you accomplish a lot of those things you will find confidence to take ownership of your life. Sometimes the best part about losing yourself is finding yourself again. You will be able to create and build on the foundations you already have to be the woman you aspire to be.

Identifying the good and the bad traits within ourselves isn't always pleasant – it can be more confronting than anything, but we ALL have them. Being self-aware will allow you control and focus on maintaining a balanced lifestyle. If we are consciously aware of our weaknesses we tend to keep them in the shadows and hidden from the judgment of others, when really we should be shining the light on our darker side. We are driven by emotions such as anger, sensitivity, anxiety and selfishness. They create opportunities to grow and achieve. Anger sparks motivation and creativity, anxiety or self-doubt can improve performance and selfishness enhances confidence. It is all about your mindset. Acknowledge and appreciate your strengths. Change your mindset and you will change your life. When you embrace yourself and all that you are, you will shine from the inside out. Everything starts to fall into place. So next time you drop your child off at the daycare centre, you'll be that woman every other mum envies because you will be glowing from the inside out, so content and confident with who you are.

In the midst of exploring the new you, do not be surprised if your old tendencies come back into play. This is because your mind has been conditioned to old behaviours and thinking patterns. Do not be disheartened or discouraged if you make a mistake and totally f**k up. These things happen, and sometimes they need to happen to remind you that the old road you were going down is not for you. Making mistakes does not mean you're failing, it means you're trying and learning in life. Forgive yourself and take the time to actually get to know you. The good, the bad and the ugly.

Another important part is having 'me time' and no, your child's nap time does not count. I struggled with this because I didn't have a lot of people around or close to me that I felt comfortable leaving my child with. To find yourself, you have to be with yourself (and yourself alone) every now and again, so you can actually enjoy your own presence without the stress of thinking about what your kids are doing if they stay quiet longer than five minutes. Put your children in daycare or have a friend or family member look after them for a few hours so you can debrief and realign. I can imagine how quickly the rush of 'mother's guilt' came over you. Don't be afraid or hold bad feelings about putting your child in care to give yourself the time you need. It is not you being selfish, it is you taking care of yourself and your mental/physical wellbeing. An unstable mother leads to an unstable family life. For me, daycare has been a positive experience. My child gets to interact with children her age, develop her learning/educational skills and be prepared to face the real world. I still recall her singing her ABCs when she was two years old and I stood there in utter shock! It still amazes me the things she has accomplished and learnt from going to daycare. So don't let the guilty feeling come over you. Taking time for you will be beneficial for you and your child(ren).

Use this time to meditate, work on your personal goals, go for a stroll along the beach or even just let your favourite candles burn while you lie star-fished on the bed. Anything that helps you zone out and feel like a twenty-something woman again. When you feel balanced and de-stressed, you will be a much calmer and happier person, and an even better mum then you already are. Being constantly stressed and overwhelmed will make everything seem harder. Nasty Mama will seem to have a longer-then-usual stay in the household and you will find yourself screaming at your kids, then crying about it later because you feel guilty. The smallest tasks will seem impossible and you will find yourself breaking down again. We all need our personal space. Isolation is the only way we can ever get to know our true self.

When you think of yourself and who you are, stay away from defining yourself by what society deems you to be. I am guilty of doing this to myself and to others. Before I had children, when people said they were a single mother I would straight away develop an imaginary picture and opinion of who they were and the life they lived, thinking they drained Centrelink of benefits and sat at home all day doing nothing. Bitch, right? Totally, and unfortunately many people do think that way. After I became a single mother, I understood that sometimes the life we are given is not always what we wanted and strived for. I pictured my happy little family with a husband who worked nine to five while I stayed at home looking after our babies in a two-storey house near the beach with a fluffy white Pomeranian but life had other plans. I was so afraid to admit to myself that I was a single mother because of society's definition of who I was and the life I lived. Being a single mother does not make you less of a person, it probably makes you more. Motherhood makes you strong. Single motherhood makes you almost indestructible. You do twice the work, have twice the stress, give twice the love and have twice the pride. Create yourself and your own being, which isn't influenced by society's definition of who you should be.

Do this by accepting your situation and yourself as you are.

Finding yourself is an enlightening and extremely vulnerable experience. You will learn so many new things the more time you spend working on yourself, doing the things you want to do. It's a time to figure out what life you want to live and how you want to live it. Almost like a fresh start. You will learn how to walk away from people and situations that threaten your peace of mind, self-respect and self-worth because you know your value. Look on the bright side, you're still young. Can you imagine how much harder it would be if you were twice your age? Be the best version of you that you can be. You've only got one life and your future is not promised. Who you are is entirely up to you.

# TAKE NOTE

"Since everything is a reflection of our minds, everything can be changed by our minds"

# SELF CARE CHECKLIST

- [ ] Meditate
- [ ] Book in to get your hair and nails done
- [ ] Do a Yoga or Pilates class
- [ ] Sleep in past 8:00am
- [ ] Have a pamper day – body scrub, face mask and hair treatment
- [ ] Watch a movie (without kids)
- [ ] Go on a lunch date with a friend
- [ ] Go get a massage
- [ ] Start a detox
- [ ] Netflix and binge
- [ ] Go for a run or walk along the beach
- [ ] Plan a vacation or staycation
- [ ] Eat out for breakfast at a fancy café
- [ ] Take a long hot bath
- [ ] Go for a hike

# LOVING YOU

Self-respect, self-love and self-worth. They all start with 'self', so do not look to anyone except yourself to find them. These three values create and alter the outcomes of every situation presented to us throughout our lifetime. If you have none of them, it's almost guaranteed you will always be left with the short end of the stick, disappointed and taken advantage of. Do not try to find your self-worth through others. When you were left crying, praying to God to help you at 3am, who was there for you? You. Who felt that pain? You. Who is left with the scars? You. You have to learn how to love yourself because you are all you've got. Accept yourself – all of you. Acknowledge the amazing qualities you have and also the dark 'dragon lady' traits that you carry. For those who are thinking 'I have no amazing qualities' or 'I'm not good at anything' – STOP! There are so many qualities women fail to see in themselves. What about the way you make your child laugh by pulling the ultimate silly face, or how you can multi-task grocery shopping, texting and pushing a trolley at the same time? What about the killer latte you make with the perfect amount of milk, or the way you can manage 'mum life' when struggling through an almost-dying hangover from seven tequila shots the night before while your girlfriends sleep half the day away. These aren't big things, but it's the little things you're good at that make you unique and make you, you.

This is the moment to be selfish, take care of yourself and be the best version of you. Treat yourself to that $200 handbag you've always wanted, start an exercise regime to flatten that mummy tummy you've always been so self-conscious about and go get your fortnightly manicure/pedicure with the French tips you adore, because you deserve it. I'm not encouraging you to get into debt but what I am saying is, whatever you desire in your life, go out and get it. You could set up a separate account and put away $20 a week or fortnight to splurge on yourself. If you're like me – working full time trying to support a household – you work damned hard for your money and you will not take that money to the grave, so treat yourself. Instead of blowing all your money on new clothes and shoes for the kids (which they probably DON'T need), spend it on a treat for yourself. Give that love you give so freely to other people to yourself. You'll need it more than ever.

*"If you don't love yourself, you will always chase the people who don't love you either."*

Most of the time when someone continually mistreats you and abuses your good faith it is because you allow them to. You cannot expect someone to know your worth and respect you if you don't respect yourself. People will treat you the way you allow them to treat you and you will find yourself settling for less because you don't know how much you're worth. Do not give your time to people who do not have time for you and who don't add value to your life. You cannot find happiness in someone else. Once you find peace and love within yourself, you will notice your relationships become richer and more meaningful. The habit of clinging to whatever comes your way won't exist anymore because you will be OK with being alone.

Those people who walk in and out of your life when it's convenient for them are the ones to remove from your circle. Do not give them the option to come and go as they please. You do not work on their time, so make that choice for them, and close the door. Each time you allow them to come as they please, the more they lose respect for you. People don't value what they are allowed to continually disrespect. If someone shows you they don't care – believe them, they really don't. They are showing you their true feelings through their actions so do not turn a blind eye to it. Keep your standards high, your self-respect intact and love yourself so much that you don't 'need' anyone else. So next time you question somebody's position in your life, ask yourself, 'Do they add any value to my life?' If the answer is no, then slam that door shut and blow them a kiss.

Throughout the course of our lives, our situations change, our goals change and our values change. A lot of the time, you see your old friends and ask yourself whether you guys even have anything in common anymore. It's not a bad thing to branch out to people who can relate to your situation or lifestyle and are in similar circumstances to you. It provides such a comfort, knowing that someone can relate to how you feel and even give you valuable advice. Social media provides the ultimate opportunity to connect and interact with groups that share your interest. I have come across many mothers' groups on Facebook but if social media isn't an option for you, there are other options. I have met plenty of young single mothers at my local playground or when I wait around to pick up my child from daycare. If your child(ren) participate in sports or other activities, make an effort to start a conversation with the other mums. Put yourself out there and make connections. When you grow and evolve, your values/priorities evolve too. Don't be afraid to make changes to the people you surround yourself with.

Your children look to their biggest influencers for guidance and way of life. So loving yourself will teach them to have self-love. Protect your heart, protect your children's hearts. Lead by example in showing them what they do and don't deserve in their life by what you accept into yours and how you let others treat you.

Trust yourself. Why is it that when our intuition tells us something or we get bad vibes, we ignore it and do it anyway? If you feel like something isn't right, it probably isn't. I look back at situations I have been through and wonder why I never listened to myself in the first place. It will save you a lot of heartache and drama in the future. When you're not sure of someone, listen to your intuition, it will tell you who you can trust – you already know the truth by the way it feels. I once met a man I thought was cute, with a beautiful smile and the biggest dimples and the perfect body. He was just my type. But something wasn't right about him. I wasn't sure whether it was because I was alcohol fueled and unable walk in a straight line, but his vibe triggered that little voice in my head telling me he was hiding something. He claimed to have no girlfriend, said he worked as a personal trainer and had no social media. After that night, one of my best friends put her investigator hat on and did some research. He definitely did have social media and was in a long-standing relationship with a beautiful blonde girl – bastard! Lesson learnt – always trust yourself. Your intuition is there for a reason.

In order to fully love yourself, you need to love the skin you're in. We are all culprits for comparing ourselves to other women and how they look. We pick on ourselves for being too fat, too tall, too small, having large boobs or having none. Women are beautiful individually, you cannot compare yourself to anyone else. What you might see as 'attractive', the next person will see less favourably. You do not need validation from anybody else to believe your body is beautiful. Embrace what you have. For example, I am pretty much the captain of the 'Itty Bitty Committee'. I could almost pass as a twelve-year-old boy the way my body is built, but strangely enough, women comment on how they would die to have my body. I am left thinking, 'I would die to have your boobs and your curves, your womanly figure'. We all want what we don't have. Looks are not everything and physical appearance deteriorates with age, but it does play a big role in making us feel good about ourselves.

Confidence stems from the way we feel about ourselves, and if we are insecure about the way we look, it will show. If you want to change your body and physical appearance, that's great but ensure that whatever it is, you're doing it for you. Not for anyone else. Going through pregnancy and motherhood puts a huge strain on our physical being and we should have a whole new level of respect for the female body. We have physically grown a human being inside ourselves and carried them for nine months.

How amazing is that? So yeah, I look like a tiger naked and my toddler always asks me what those weird stripes all over my body are, but you know what? I love them because they represent my journey of motherhood, puberty, weight loss and victory.

## Five Things I Love About Myself

1.


2.

3.

4.

5.

# TAKE NOTE

"You are only confined to the walls that you build"

# THE
# NOISE

There is nothing worse than listening to people's opinions about your life situation or how you're raising your children, especially when they know nothing about the pain you've endured and are fighting through. I love how they just expect you to take on board their comments like you actually give a sh*t about what they're saying, especially because you are younger than the average mum. Noise can come from so many people around you. Your family, your in-laws, your friends and even the old lady that walks past you in the grocery shop to give her two cents' worth about how you shouldn't let your child stand on the front of the trolley. That's the thing, no matter what you do or how you do it, people are going to have opinions of you and your life no matter what. Sometimes they'll voice their opinion and sometimes they won't – well not to your face anyway…

Blocking out this noise is hard. You dwell on people's comments, think about what they said and question yourself, but if you let other people's opinions alter your life decisions, you are going to be angry at yourself when things don't work out the way they were supposed to and all you can blame is yourself. You are in charge of your own life, and you are the one who is going to have to live with the consequences of your decisions. People give advice and opinions based on their personal experiences, and usually with twist of their ego. It is all about them. No two people's life experiences are the same. People feel pain and deal with pain differently so really, no one's advice or opinion can take into consideration your reality. Not everyone is going to agree with your decisions, but remember, not everyone matters.

Every now and again we will find ourselves being flattered by positive comments and reinforcement. Not all opinions or comments are made in a negative light. These types of people are the ones to surround yourself with. The people who create a vibrant and positive environment that allows you to bounce off their energy. It's not often that we have those people in our lives but when we do it's important to keep them close. Some people will inspire you and some will drain you. You will figure out the difference very quickly.

I will never forget the awkward and uncomfortable moment I got thrown into during a social group where I was asked, 'Oh why aren't you with the father anymore?' while her head tilted slightly to the right. I couldn't think of anything worse to ask someone you hardly know but for some unknown reason I felt obliged to answer. One lesson I have learnt is that you do not have to respond to people who question why your life is the way it is. It's none of their business – pure and simple. I did answer her honestly, but soon regretted it because it made me feel judged and slightly embarrassed that things didn't work out the way I wanted them to. That is a fine example of putting yourself in a position to be criticised when it is not even necessary, especially if you are uncomfortable about answering.

Escaping the judgement of others is near impossible. So no matter how frustrated you are about constantly being picked at, analysed and talked about, it's life. It is out of your control. But what is in your control is how you let it impact you. Never judge yourself through the eyes of someone else. I can't tell you how many times I've waltzed into the office carrying my bitch-faced attitude because earlier that morning I endured a twenty-minute temper tantrum from my toddler and also spilled my hot morning coffee all down the front of my white blouse while trying to get out of the car because I was half an hour late for work. Perfect start to the day. The thing is, nobody knows that. That's one reason why you should never take anybody's judgment to heart, because they don't know the ins and outs of your life or what you went through before you rocked up to work looking like a hot mess. You should use this in your own practice too. Next time you are about to spit out that nasty comment about someone else, remember how you felt. When you judge someone else, you are defining who you are – not them. So let them talk about you, let them judge away on something they know nothing about.

TAKE NOTE

"The greatest accomplishment in life, is not never failing, but in the rising after you fall"

# DREAM AND INSPIRE

An essential part of building your life and yourself is to set goals, dream big and be inspired. The world is yours to conquer and nothing is unachievable. Your mind-set creates possibilities and sets boundaries. Do not let your mind build walls that do not exist. You only have one chance in this life to be whatever it is you want to be. Nobody can tell you that you can't, except you! Think about what you really wanted to achieve or become but never knew how or where to start, which completely turned you off the entire idea. That is what you should be working on, striving for and aspiring to achieve every single day.

Surround yourself with people who make you want to be better or do better. People who inspire you to want to build on the person you are already. Inspiration and energy is contagious. Don't be afraid of what could go wrong, and get excited about what could go right. When you think about setting goals, you can start with small ones – they don't always have to be big and extravagant like getting hitched to George Clooney and spending the rest of your life as a 'lady of leisure'. The little things, like doing exercise a few times a week or toilet training your toddler. Everyone has to start somewhere, people aren't born successful, they work hard to achieve it. Little goals will soon turn into big goals, and when we accomplish our goals, we have a sense of achievement which then reflects in our self-esteem.

Take a look at JK Rowling's story; we all know her as the writer of the famous Harry Potter books. She had a young daughter, was reportedly abused by her husband, divorced and diagnosed with severe depression all by the time she was twenty-eight. She became a single mother living on welfare when she was twenty-nine and contemplated suicide. She put all her energy and passion into doing something she loved and by the age of forty-one she had sold millions of copies of her book and become a success. If that doesn't inspire you, then I don't know what will.

Never give up on your dreams; it is never too late and never too hard to start working on them. Give yourself the chance to accomplish what you thought you couldn't. What better time than now to start?

People around you aren't always going to be supportive of your dreams and aspirations. Not everyone is cheering for you on the sidelines and unfortunately sometimes it's the people closest to us who are praying for our failure. Don't worry about the ones who aren't happy for you, they probably aren't happy for themselves either. Ignore the people who try to bring you down. Focus on you. Your life is about outgrowing yourself and breaking your limits. You are not in competition with anyone except yourself. You are pushing through one of the hardest challenges life can offer. Motherhood is tough and doing it alone is something to be proud of. A single mother who chases her dreams and has aspirations to change her life? Now that's bad-ass.

## TAKE NOTE

"At first they'll ask you why you're doing it, but after they'll ask you how you did it"

# DREAM AND INSPIRE

# NEVER GIVE UP

No matter how hard things get, never give up. Something will grow from all the pain you're going through, and that will be you. Many times I thought about throwing in the towel and giving up because life was 'too hard' but didn't. In the end, you will look back and wonder how you ever made it to where you are now.

Don't give up on you, because someone else gave up on you. No matter who you lose in your life, never lose yourself.

You will encounter setbacks and plenty of hiccups along the way, but never stop moving forward. Before you think about giving up, think about why you held on so long. Think about everything you ever stood for and all the people who doubted you. Nothing worth having comes easily. Your greatest moments in life are yet to come so don't throw away all your hard work because you hit a rock on the way. If you need a break, take one, but never quit. Quitting is the easy way out. Not only am I talking in terms of achieving your personal goals, but with life in general. If you want to kill yourself, kill the woman you used to be, and build the woman you want to be. Nobody in the world is perfect or has a perfect past. We have all done things we aren't particularly proud of and said things we wish we could take back but that is life. We are human beings, we grow and learn about life through our experiences. The only important thing is what we learnt and took away from each situation.

If you're not a spiritual or religious person, this might be hard to relate to, but I am a strong believer that God will only give his toughest battles to those he knows can conquer them. If you pray and ask for something consistently it will be given to you. Take each day with gratitude and use the Law of Attraction to stay positive. The more you focus on something, the more powerful it becomes and you can make good things happen more quickly by thinking about them. Life has a funny way of always working out, you just need believe and have faith that you are exactly where you are meant to be in this moment.

Everything you need to reach your goals in life is inside you. Life has many challenges and everyone is battling something. Everyone's life has a time span, tomorrow isn't a given. One day you are going to be that woman who younger girls look up to and aspire to be like. You've had all the odds against you, and you still succeeded. What a woman. Sometimes our blessings are disguised. What might seem like nightmare will lead you to your biggest dream. Believe in yourself and all that you are. You were born for this.

# TAKE NOTE

*When I feel like giving up, this is what I will tell myself:*

NEVER GIVE UP

# THANK YOU

## For Meegan
### 1991-2017

*Thank you for always seeing the best in me.*
*You are forever and always in my heart.*

This book was written in the loving memory of my close friend Meegan, who passed away at the age of twenty-five, leaving two young children. Her passing has inspired me to write about the struggles and heartbreak that come with being a young single mother in today's society. I became a single parent at the age of twenty-three. I was married at twenty-two, fell pregnant with a little girl and had my life perfectly planned out, but when things didn't go as expected, I became lost, empty and broken. Everything in my life became frustrating and I couldn't seem to find that happiness everyone else so easily seemed to have. I looked for happiness in everyone else except myself.

After Meegan's passing, I made a promise that I would never take my life for granted and I would appreciate everything I had in this lifetime. I welcomed all my emotions that I used to push away, while learning to love myself the way I was, flaws and all! It was the most enlightening and life-changing experience. Finding peace within myself opened me up to a whole new world. I became happier and lived a more fulfilled lifestyle with my daughter. This book will give you an insight into my journey and the stages I went through transforming my life.

The most precious thing we have on this earth is time. Give your time to people and things that are important, that serve you and that will help you grow. Most of the time, we bury all the problems, the pain and the heartache because we are afraid of how much it will hurt when it surfaces. And when it does come to the surface, you hit rock bottom, and you don't know what do to with yourself. You panic to find someone to help you or tell you what to do to fix your life. So I have written this book in hope that it reaches out to the women and young single mothers who feel like they're falling apart, who don't have their sh*t together, and to let them know there is hope. You will survive, it will get better and you will come out on top. Pushing through the emotional rollercoaster of heartbreak and single parenting isn't easy. I hope this book will support and guide you in getting through this rough patch in your life.

Thank you to all my beautiful friends who have been by my side through everything – without you I wouldn't be where I am today. To Kate Stagg from Parklife Group and Karen McDermott from Karen McDermott Publishing for encouraging me to write this book and being my support network through the whole process. To my bosses, Paul and Kylie Flannery for putting up with my mid-week mental breakdowns and being the best bosses on the planet! And lastly to my little girl, thank you for choosing me to be your mummy. You have taught me so much about life and who I am.

www.ingramcontent.com/pod-product-compliance
Lightning Source LLC
Chambersburg PA
CBHW042051290426
44110CB00001B/27